Confessions of a Divorce Lawyer
A Must Read for Divorce

Timothy R. Ash, Esq

Confessions of a Divorce Lawyer

Independently Published

Copyright © 2020, Timothy R. Ash, Esq

Published in the United States of America

200217-01544.2

ISBN: 9798647966629

No parts of this publication may be reproduced without correct attribution to the author of this book.
For more information on 90-Minute Books including finding out how you can publish your own book, visit 90minutebooks.com or call (863) 318-0464

Here's What's Inside...

Upfront 1

Introduction 4

Chapter One
What Law School Teaches You 10

Chapter 2
Life's Twisting Turns 15

Chapter Three
Living on the Edge! 23

Chapter Four
Here Comes the Judge 29

Chapter Five
The Final Fall 36

Chapter Six
Finding Blessings in Unusual Places 40

Chapter Seven
So Long, Self 49

Chapter Eight
Divorce Done the Right Way 53

Chapter Nine
So Your Spouse Isn't Playing Fair 69

Chapter Ten
Go the Distance 76

Chapter Eleven
My Advice to You 81

Chapter Twelve
This Could Change the World 88

Chapter Thirteen
It's Worth It! 92

Epilogue 97

Upfront

If you are thinking of getting a divorce or you have already been served divorce papers, there are things you need to know before you wade in. If you do not take a moment to address these concerns, you will be vulnerable and blindsided by forces that you did not foresee.

I want to mention an approach to your divorce that I'll share more once we get into the book. First, getting a divorce is going to be painful, no matter what you do. You cannot live with someone and create a home and dreams for the future, but not feel hurt when it all falls apart. But the way you approach the pain will either leave you strengthened to withstand troubles or leave you vulnerable, with your life crumbling around you. We'll review more about having a strong foundation versus a foundation made of sand, subject to your vulnerabilities, as you study the following pages.

Second, you can go through a process that will help you come out on the other side of this divorce, transformed with a healthy vision, and hope for the future. What is the alternative? The answer is a destructive divorce that leaves you suffering from post-traumatic stress syndrome (PTSD). Too many times (and I'm sure you've heard this too), 20 years after a divorce, the parties are still bitter and hateful towards their spouse and, in many cases, hateful towards the world.

What a waste of precious life!

If you want to have a transformed life full of hope and love after your divorce, you need to keep from falling into the trap of hate, being unforgiving, shame, regret, and bitterness. One of the ways to protect yourself is to discover how you can bring your emotions under control. Whether the predominant emotions are anger, hurt, betrayal, or rage, these can be managed through love, forgiveness, and integrity. In the end, the process you are about to read through will equip you to deal with your divorce while keeping a strong attitude for resolution, and a clear vision towards planning a bright future. Not only is this for yourself, but it will enable you to exit your marriage while taking to heart what is truly best for your children.

When it comes to marriage and divorce, neither one is easy; people will be hurt in the process. With the proper system and guidance in place, you don't need to end up a wounded victim for the rest of your life. You've got too much good life left to live, so don't sign it all over during the divorce proceedings. Let's go through this together.

By your side,

Tim

Introduction

I was a small-town boy, fortunate enough to be brought up in a tightknit, caring family. My mom loved everything about our small town, especially being out in the country; nothing made her happier than raising her show horses. But my dad, he loved the big city. It's kind of funny, now that I think of it that my life mirrored my favorite television show. Every afternoon, my favorite time of day was when I could lay on my stomach in the middle of the living room and watch *Green Acres*. I could see our little family as the main characters, but just flipped around!

I guess you could say I was born with the blood of an entrepreneur; my dad was a full-time financial planner. Really, *his* daily habits modeled to me what it looked like to be your own boss.

Once or twice a year, he would win exotic trips and take the entire family. I was so excited; I could hardly wait to see these amazing far-away places like Florida or Las Vegas. Those trips felt like a great adventure; I remember looking out the car window as we drove from Bath, Michigan to sunny California. The trip took a month because, of course, my brother and I were kids, and had to stop all along the way to see all the roadside parks and scenic viewpoints. We kids had great fun in the back seat, mixed with quite a bit of teasing! It was an amazing time in my life.

Unfortunately, when we returned to school, all the kids picked on me because of my dark tan. They would say my dad was rich, and I didn't belong at that school.

Those were hard years; the elementary and middle school years were especially rough on me. But as they say, there's always a silver lining. Everything changed in high school when the most beautiful girl in school started paying attention to me. I couldn't believe it! She started just asking me questions about my homework. Being an insecure teenager, I thought she was just interested in me for my homework answers. In retrospect, I laugh because, to tell the truth, I was a lousy student! Once I finally caught on that she was flirting with me, soon after we began dating.

As time went on, I realized what different lives we had lived. She was much more advanced in life for her age. Sadly, her parents had gone through a difficult divorce when she was young, and the consequences had really affected her. I always felt bad for her because my home life was so different, more like *Leave It to Beaver.* All my family members were devoted Catholics. If you ever needed to get ahold of my family on a Sunday, you could always find us parked together on a pew in church.

As our relationship continued, like most teenagers, we began having many discussions surrounding sex. I was still a virgin in high school since I was devoted to my Catholic faith. But like many kids my age, my passions eventually overtook my devotion to the church. My crush gave way and blossomed into full-blown puppy love, and at age 15, I lost my virginity. As our senior year ended, my life looked like it was just getting started. Everything changed in an instant. With tears in her eyes and fear in her voice, my high school sweetheart told me she was pregnant.

But, wait a minute, this book isn't about me, it's about YOU! (You'll see in a moment why I'm telling you my deep, dark secrets.) You see, I have a hidden hope for you. My heartfelt hope is that you learn more about yourself and what you really want for this next part of your life as you read my true confessions.

Life as I Knew It Ended

In that split second, my life not only turned upside down, but it got knotted up in my stomach until I felt like I would drown. As badly as I felt, that I had just ruined my life, now I had to face the two people who loved me most. For years these two people had encouraged me; they had dreams and goals for me. I had to shatter their world with the same words that were drowning me. As I write this and think back to that day, I still feel the pain of it. Telling my parents was absolutely brutal. My mom, who never drank, got drunk on Boones Farm and began throwing up. My true confession didn't go over very well with my dad, either. As a young Catholic, I decided the only choice was to get married.

So, we got married…and divorced…all in the first year! My high school sweetheart and mother of my child left me for another guy. I say this in a few short, sharp sentences to end it quickly—but the pain, hate, anger, bitterness, rejection, and embarrassment I felt at that time, ended up lasting over three decades. I had no choice but to gather up our child and move back home in shame.

The amazing thing is that it would take 34 years and a 45-minute conversation with my ex-wife to let go of all those years of built-up hurt. All the years of grief and rage that I had buried, but still haunted me, being so unforgiving and the feeling of betrayal that I dragged around with me, weighing me down like a cinderblock tied around my neck. In that one moment and one conversation, it was all gone. You see, at that moment, I experienced the healing POWER of transformation in my life. I offer this book as a way for you to start your own transformation. Whether you are heading towards divorce, you're in the middle of one, or you have been holding on to past hurts, this book is for you. I often tell my clients, "There is only one thing worse than divorce; it's the wreckage it leaves behind."

A Win/Lose Proposition

Our court system and yes, even the attorneys, approach the *divorce process* as a win/lose proposition. Of course, everyone wants to win, but that means there needs to be someone who loses. Typically, when the couple starts talking to their family, friends, and work associates, they discover they are the ones losing.

It's always so sad to hear well-meaning friends say, "You need to hire a lawyer and fight this thing." That is their natural response and what they are coached to do. Of course, this stirs the pot of an already highly emotional situation. By the time both parties get to their attorneys, they are boiling over with anger; they are only focused on hurting their spouse.

The problem with that approach is you will still need to bury the hatchet at the end of the divorce. And while you're burying your hatchet, you'll need to try and bury all your emotions and let all the pain go as well. Believe me, without help, that's a tall order to fill.

After that, the next thing your well-meaning friends will tell you is this: "Okay, the divorce is over; go out and get on with your life." Really? Just like that?

After all the fighting and hurt, the last thing you want to do is *get on with your life*; what you really want to do is crawl in a hole. Let me reassure you that it doesn't have to be that way. You truly can come out of your divorce and go on to live a happy, fulfilled, free life. You don't have to drag around your bitterness and hurt for over three decades like I did. You don't have to end your marriage with a divorce that gives you both PTSD! There's a better way.

Let's face this thing together,

Tim

Chapter One
What Law School Teaches You

Though I wasn't a very good student, I can't say I flunked everything because there was one thing I did love about school—lunch! Apparently, that wasn't very impressive to my mom. She got super negative with me when I started to tell her I was going to law school. I can still see the disbelief all over her face. She couldn't even hide how shocked she was to hear I was going to law school. That's not a good feeling when your mom thinks you're joking about something like that. She said, "Tim, get serious, you can't even spell attorney!"

At that moment, something shifted deep inside of me. I felt like a giant boulder had dropped off the side of a cliff and landed in the pit of my stomach. It was a staggering experience. I made a decision that would change the course of my life. I decided then and there that I was going to prove all of them wrong!

My grandfather believed in me so much so that he provided the seed money that would take me through my first year of law school. My wife and I were both working full-time, and our goal was to get through law school without any student loans. We knew this would be difficult with a small child and all the daycare bills, but we were determined.

Reality Sets In... With a Thud!

So I was all jazzed up to prove everybody wrong, to prove I could be the world's greatest attorney. Then I realized that I really had a huge obstacle to overcome. What was I thinking? The deck was stacked against me. I was not a very good student back in high school or college. Now I had grown into a man with a second marriage and a young child. I knew that becoming an attorney was going to be the hardest thing I would ever do. I already had a lot happening in my life; I was still working full-time for Michigan National Corporation, applying to go to law school, and raising a child. That gives me a headache just thinking about it. I had so much to learn and so much to prove, not only to everyone else but to myself. This was my chance

Surprise! I Started Failing Law School

My first semester had gone really well; I felt like I had the tiger by the tail. I was very busy patting myself on the back for the great job I had done… and then came the second semester. In class, as part of our practice to be in court, we would do mock arguments. One day, I got to do a closing argument in front of 100 people. I was on top of the world. It was funny that just months earlier, I had doubted my dream. One fellow student said I was the next Jeffrey Fieger. That felt good to hear; he was a successful attorney.

Just when I thought I was going to breeze through law school, the third semester hit me like a load of bricks dropped out of a B-52 airplane. The reality of the difficulty of life and law school reared its ugly head; I suddenly had a big problem with my grades. The problem was named D & F. You can't get much worse than that.

I ended up on academic probation. I absolutely could not believe it. I had really let myself down. But just because I dug myself into a hole, I wasn't about to stay down there. I devised a plan to dig myself out. I got the sample answers for the class exam I had failed. When I was reviewing it, I found a question that I believed I answered correctly. So I appealed to the professor's decision.

**Fighting for My Life...
At Least That's the Way It Felt!**

The appeal process required that I argue my point to a fellow student. The student was persuaded by my position, so my appeal advanced to the second round. Next, I had to argue in front of a student panel. I had to square off against a student who was advocating for the professor. After the argument, I really felt like I did a pretty good job. But the next round was out of my hands; the panel took their opinion to the professor.

All I could do at that point was to wait. The whole long, drawn-out process ended up taking two semesters, and for the entire time, I continued to be on academic probation. I still remember the instructor's name was Nedium. You don't know how many times I heard from other students, "You're wasting your time, buddy; Nedium has never reversed a grade. Ever!"

Two semesters later, the results of my appeal were posted. Before I had a chance to see the results, my friends were patting me on the back, congratulating me for doing the impossible. Nedium had reversed the grade! I was empowered and felt unstoppable. The world threw me a 90-mph curveball, and I hit it out of the park. There was nothing I could not do; I was on top of the world. I had fallen into a deep dark hole, and I refused to give up. I kept positive and never gave up hope.

*When you feel that you are about to fall,
it might actually be that you are about to FLY*

Chapter 2
Life's Twisting Turns

It was my big break! My wife was selling Yellow Pages on commission. The corporate office in Troy, Michigan, offered her a marketing position with a salary and bonuses. This offered us financial stability! The timing was perfect, as I was offered a buyout with Michigan National Corporation, and I was starting my second year of law school. I would have to commute to Lansing, but we knew as a family, it was the right thing to do.

They say behind every great man is a wonderful, strong, and loving woman. At least the latter is correct. My wife provided the income to make law school possible, and if the truth is known, nearly 100% of the nurturing and being there for our child was my wife, a child that she adopted as her own without reservation. I remember baseball games. I was in the stands with my nose in a book. My wife would elbow me when our child was about to make a play or was up to bat.

We Loaded Up the Truck and Moved to White Lake.

My wife's promotion allowed me to focus on a job better suited to my legal education. I sent out resumes for a clerk position, including the Oakland County circuit court, and quickly found an opportunity to interview for a court clerk position. For the first time, I felt in control and finally able to seek out my legal destiny. When I met Judge Gilbert, that meeting turned out to be one of the biggest blessings of my law school career. She took me under her wing, giving me a job as her clerk and inspiring me towards a love for the law.

The courthouse where I worked with Judge Gilbert was only 20 minutes from home, and an hour and a half from law school; it was perfect for night classes. With the reversal of my grade from an E to a C, I was able to get off the academic probation list; from there on out, my grades soared. I fell head over heels in love with the law. I was learning law and seeing its application every day at my job. It was an amazing time in my life.

Murder and Mayhem

I was hired in October of 1989. In November, Judge Gilbert presided over a five-week murder trial. One month after being hired, I was sitting next to the Judge, calling the case, swearing in witnesses, and managing reporters. I saw the most outstanding prosecutor and three high-profile defense attorneys at their craft. The skill at which they worked provided me with an outstanding education. The arguments were pure magic. I drank them up like a deer pants for streams of water. I took every opportunity to discuss strategy and style with each attorney. As the court's clerk, I received special treatment.

It was the prosecutor's position that the defendant had his wife kidnapped from a grocery store and murdered her. The prosecutor claimed he had carved up her body, placing her remains in three garbage bags, which were discovered in a ravine. Every day, throughout the trial, there were three cameras strategically situated in the courtroom; the presence of the cameramen gave the whole process an air of excitement. Having the opportunity to see justice served was a dream come true.

My Entire World Became the Courtroom.

My wife and I would join the attorneys after court on Fridays at their favorite watering hole. It really felt like we were on top of the world. Within a short time, Judge Gilbert hosted another high-profile trial; this time, it was Dr. Kevorkian (Dr. Death). The doctor was represented by Jeffrey Fieger, who had some recognition, but it was his representation of Dr. Kevorkian that made him famous and nationally known.

I learned so much from law school, from my experience with Judge Gilbert and other judges. In my third year of law school, with six months until graduation, Judge Gilbert announced she was running for Congress. Of course, I was excited for her, but that left me unsure of my job. The court clerks were a tight group, especially the clerks attending law school; Ken, who clerked for Judge Rudy Nichols, let me know he was leaving. I quickly put in my resume and was hired.

It was very educational to learn that Judge Nichols did not handle his docket in the same way as Judge Gilbert. Judge Nichols allowed me to brief motions and meet with attorneys. He was an amazing teacher and person. I worked for him until I graduated. Unfortunately, his senior clerk (Paul) was taking the Bar Exam at the same time as I was, and the Judge had to let me go.

I was looking forward to the extra time for studying when I received a call; there was a position open to clerk for Judge Anderson. I jumped at the chance to work for another judge—who wouldn't!

I still remember the interview; I mentioned that I was taking the bar exam. The Judge kicked back in his chair; he was up in years, and chuckled, "Bar exam." He went on, "It's kind of like an AIDS test—pass it, no big deal, but fail it and..." his whole body shivered. I asked him for four weeks to study; he gave me two instead.

Top Gun

Two weeks may seem like a long time to study for the bar exam; it wasn't! I graduated in January 1993 and sat for the bar examination that February. I took a prep class, as was common, at night after I got out of work. The education and understanding of how the three judges handled their cases further improved my resume. Initially, my time was focused on preparing for the bar. I did the best to keep up on the coursework and prepare for what I would later refer to as 'D-day.' By the time it came down to two weeks, I had to study 12 hours a day. At the end of each day, I would watch the movie *Top Gun* to settle down and go to sleep.

'D-day' came and went. I knew I got at least three of the 200 questions right, and I was pretty confident in my essay answers. It would be four months until I would find out. I took the next four months to learn from Judge Anderson and envisioned becoming a lawyer. It was a weekday when Paul called the Judge's chamber. "Tim, did you hear so and so got his results, he passed." My heart was immediately racing, and I thought I was going to be sick. I knew the day was coming, but now it was here. We both exclaimed that our mail did not come until the afternoon. We agreed to meet for a drinking lunch. When I returned, the Judge's secretary (Ann) could not hide the evidence. I said, "You know." She could hardly say she didn't and said that I needed to call my wife. If you have ever felt like your life came down to a moment, this was it for me.

Holding My Breath

I called, and my wife answered. I said, "Did I pass?" She said—as if she knew it all along—"You passed." I inquired if she was home, and she stated that she was at work. I asked how she found out, and she told me that she sent our 11-year-old son to the mailbox. The part we will never forget is the way he read the result. He said, "Mom, it says PA55."

Fill out the following questions, be as specific as possible. (Use extra paper if necessary.)

1. At which times in your marriage did you feel on top of the world?

2. Write down why they made you feel that way.

3. Were they realistic?

4. Write down the times when you put the responsibility of your happiness on your spouse.

5. How did you feel when they disappointed you?

6. What did you do with those feelings?

Chapter Three
Living on the Edge!

Shortly after I turned 30 years old in 1992, my wife and I had our first son together. By 1995 our family had grown, and I was now a happy husband and father of three children, or as I call them, the Three Musketeers. Today, they are adults and have homes of their own, but I'm still over the moon when we get together, and I see their closeness; their love radiates. My brother and I are blessed to have the same relationship with love at the center, even with families and our busy schedules. We always make time to invest in our relationships.

As Perfect as My Life Sounds, All Was Not As It Seemed

I wanted to work for the prosecutor's office, but they turned me down. That turned out to be a good thing because it left me with an even stronger desire to prove myself. I felt that working for a firm would not fulfill my need for success, so I started my own practice. I went to all the judges and staff and began accepting court-appointed defendants to represent. This turned out to be quite lucrative, and within a short time, I was conducting jury trials.

About a year after I got my license, a friend told me that a friend of his had killed his wife with a hammer; this was all over the news. He asked if I could see his friend while he was being held in jail, and I said, "Yes." The defendant's name was Raymond Ponke; at the end of the meeting, he asked if I would represent him. So I set off to do my interviews. I had a sneaking suspicion this wasn't a cut-and-dried case.

After many hours of research and talking to Raymond's friends and family, I thought I had it figured out. I went to St. Louis to meet with a world-renowned expert on Huntington's disease. After interviewing her, I decided to retain her to testify that Ray had Huntington's disease and that the disease made him kill his wife.

Messiah Complex

For the first time, I felt my life was really starting to build momentum. I was getting good cases and making great money. This was all very exciting, but it left an even stronger desire to prove myself. You can imagine, with all this confidence-building me up, how I felt when the jury returned a verdict of guilty. My desire to prove myself was coming at a HUGE COST! I only saw the verdict as affecting me and passing judgment on my performance; I did not even think of Ray or his family. The thought never entered my mind about Huntington's disease, how gruesome it was, and how it had destroyed the Ponke family. If you have a parent with Huntington's, you have a 50% chance of being born with the gene. However, the symptoms do not show up until middle age.

When I represented Ray, researchers had just developed a way to determine if you had the gene. For all the years prior to that, all you could do was to wait and see if the symptoms showed up. Huntington's disease is brutal; it affects the person physically, mentally, and emotionally. The person continues to function all the while the disease is destroying them until they end up in a fetal position, malnourished, and waiting for death.

Thinking back on that time in my life, I see how selfish I was. It is mind-boggling that I was so caught up in my own desires to be successful, to prove to everyone that I could win and save the world, instead of realizing there wasn't anything I could do to save Ray or his family and allowing myself to sit with that pain and sadness. My drive for success continued. I saved some money and put it down on a Yellow Pages ad for criminal and divorce clients. At this point, I had two associates, and the firm was beginning to grow. I realized that divorce customers were more lucrative, and it gave me a sense of purpose after having gone through my own divorce.

The firm grew exponentially, and so did my head. I purchased a BMW 740i, some Michael Flohr paintings, a yacht, built an elegant home, and the children wanted for nothing. My wife proudly displayed her four-carat diamond wedding ring and a closet full of fine shoes and ornate clothes. I had a six-figure line of credit, and we were never denied a credit card. I decided I needed some more toys, so I purchased a Corvette, a Harley, and a couple of snowmobiles; I felt guilty, so we got a puppy for the kids. We went on extravagant trips and lived a lavish lifestyle.

One of my favorite memories is of a boat trip with a group of fellow Sea Ray owners to the North Channel. Ten days of heaven. Every day was full of adventure and excitement! At the mid-week point, it was time to lower our lifeboats and put them to the test. A rally course was marked, which required precision as we navigated through the rocks—riding in a rubber raft powered by an outboard so powerful that the boat planes, it is quite an experience. Halfway through the course was lunch, and a full bar set up on the rocks. We enjoyed fresh-cooked fish and cocktails. It was perfect. In the evening, it was dueling pianos and lots of singing. I still love going through the photos we took.

Fill out the following questions, be as specific as possible. (Use extra paper if necessary.)

1. Have you placed unrealistic expectations on yourself?

2. Describe the event in your life that has been most disappointing.

3. How has this event affected how you live your life today?

Chapter Four
Here Comes the Judge

The decision to purchase a full-page Yellow Pages ad and going into divorce law tripled my business. Of course, all my expenses boomed as well. But I thought I could do no wrong. I enjoyed spending all my discretionary income that came from the 30 to 45 clients I worked with each month. It all began to feed on itself, as unbridled success often can. I had never seen money like this before, and of course, I wanted to enjoy the good life.

Humpty Dumpty Took a Big Fall

Looking back on that time in my life, now I see the real fragility of my puffed-up life of luxury. A recurrent memory from my younger life comes to me whenever I feel trapped. At about ten years old, I had this friend named Steve, who had a fiberglass boat; we called it a dinghy with a small outboard engine. One day my brother and I went for a ride with Steve, who was three or four years older. My dad did not know; we were afraid that if we asked to go, he would say no. So we set off on Lake Macatawa in Holland, Michigan. Steve took us to an area where the lake was open, then it narrowed, and then it opened again.

There was a reason why he went there; the best waves were there, and we wanted to hit them with the dinghy. We were having so much fun, laughing, singing, and enjoying ourselves. The waves were crashing into the boat, which, of course, was the point until one of us noticed that the boat was filling with water. We started bailing, but our shifting weight was causing more water to get in than we were able to bail out. It was so scary. We decided to stay still and head for shore.

"Please, no more waves," we pleaded. A few hit here and there. The boat was filled almost to the top, and total fear set in. We saw the shore; we could make it! Just then, a boat cruised by. I do not know what it would have felt like on the Titanic when that big boat disappeared into the sea, but I do know the absolute panic and fear I felt as a young boy, experiencing that boat disappear from under me. This story is repeated in my life every time I feel life slipping out of control. When I was 45 years old, I could feel my boat filling to the brim, and I was going down.

Good Money After Bad

From living the good life and rewarding myself for all of my hard work, I started experiencing some financial issues from spending more than I was making and taking advantage of the credit I had gained. I took some of my income, and instead of paying off debt, I invested it so I could have even more money without the financial issues. I got into some real estate investments in hopes that it would be the answer to my financial crisis. Of course, I had to go into bigger debt to finance my new investments. Having seen some success with my real estate investments, I decided, even though I had zero experience, to invest in a cosmetic surgery center.

To get the word out, I had to double my advertising budget to advertise for my law practice and the cosmetic surgery center. By the time 2008 and 2009 rolled around, I ended up losing $200,000 dollars in liens, but the storm was just getting started. When I look back at that time in my life, I now realize that my clients, my colleagues, and the court system were my proving ground. I looked at the car I drove, the office where I worked, the house, my children's clothes, and school—everything I did was to prove myself. At this stage, proving myself as a lawyer meant proving to the client I was better than all the other attorneys.

Little focus was placed on how to serve clients, just how to tell them what they wanted to hear—what it took to retain me as their attorney. Little thought or concern was given to the actual problems that clients were facing. The focus was control—stay in control of the client's wants and desires, stay in control of what the opposing attorney is doing, and don't let the court control the process. More than a few times, this strategy fell apart; each time, it caused me to bring harm to myself and everyone around me, including those I loved the most: my wife and children. Everyone masks pain, shame, and guilt differently; for me, they were masked through self-destructive behaviors that made me feel better about myself. In these times, the economy and truth properly waged a war that brought me to my knees.

It All Came Tumbling Down

All the money that came in from the law practice was now in the process of being consumed by debt payments. I thought my only answer was to continue to borrow money, so I could continue to live my lavish lifestyle. So, what's the problem with continuing to borrow money? *The problem is there is never enough to fill the hole if you keep on digging!* By 2010, the good times had left the building. All of my lines of credit were canceled. Since I had been servicing my other loans with part of that money, I was left in a very bad spot.

But Wait... It Gets Worse

Remember all those real estate deals? They were my rental properties. By 2010, all of my investment properties were sitting vacant. At that time, my old familiar feeling of deep, dark failure began to sneak back in, the one I had when my high school sweetheart got pregnant. That familiar dark feeling came in gently. It happened slowly, almost like storm clouds quietly rolling in, ominous and threatening. You don't see them until your world begins to grow dark. The more my lifestyle raged out of control, the harder I tried to get my life back into control. I borrowed against our house, my business, and credit cards investing in businesses; I purchased rental homes and made risky loans with high returns to keep my lifestyle in place. I remember I was in Judge Grant's courtroom when the Judge announced, "We are under attack." We all remember where we were when the Twin Towers went down, but it's ironic that I can't remember where I was or when I made all these devastating decisions that wrecked my life.

The innocent victims were my wife and children. I was destroying my life, but they were going down with me. Let this be a message to you— never forget that what you do has a significant effect on those who are closest to you. I was destroying my life, but my anxiety escalated when I considered how my actions would look to others. I remember sitting on our gorgeous boat, shaking with fear and uncertainty. I had gambled a huge amount of debt on some plans that were not panning out. I was on this runaway train, with troubles appearing on every front. My kids hated me. I had divorce papers written up. I ran into State Bar problems. Bankruptcy was imminent. It was all just too much!

Admitting Failure Was the Hardest Part

I had done everything my foolish mind could think to do, and yet at every turn, my bad decisions were exposing the truth. In 2008 and 2009, property values were cut in half. My divorce business relied heavily on the final payment coming from the sale, or a lien placed upon the marital home. I would collect a modest retainer, and as the fees would accumulate, I would rely on the lien to get paid. When property values plummeted, I lost over $200,000 in liens and other receivables from notices of bankruptcy. I was spending $7,000 to $12,000 just in advertising. Rent, payroll, and other expenses were greater than our income.

Fill out the following questions, be as specific as possible. (Use extra paper if necessary.)

1. Was there a time when everything came crashing down on you?

2. How did you respond?

3. Were you defensive when it happened?

4. Did you blame everyone except yourself?

5. Are you defensive now?

Chapter Five
The Final Fall

In 2011, the hole I had dug got very real, very fast. I ended up in the office of my good friend, discussing options. My wife and I gave the grim details. Our overspending, mortgages on the rentals, loans on business deals that had gone badly, and overspending on advertising for the divorce practice put us in an impossible situation. Even though my wife was making a good salary, it wasn't enough, but it was enough to keep us from filing Chapter 7; it was suggested that we file Chapter 13. But it was just the beginning; I was finally ready to take responsibility for my financial irresponsibility.

A New Start

Going through the bankruptcy process really broke through my pride, but in a good way. After we set up the bankruptcy, something surprising happened. I was filled with new hope; it just flooded my whole body. In my suffering, the transformation was born. I was introduced to a men's group called Doorkeepers, and I've been a part of the ministry for a decade. The two men who lead the group are truly a gift to me as well as all the wonderful men I have grown to love. Many times over the years, I have been out of this country with this group on mission trips. We meet every Tuesday night and Friday mornings to share our faith in Jesus. These are very special men who love in a very special way.

The impact these men have had on me is monumental—men from every side of life—doctors, lawyers, engineers, salesmen, blue-collar, white-collar, we do not discriminate. If you are hurt by a bad relationship, divorce, or death close to your heart, a group like Doorkeepers is a must. Seeing the wonderful movie, *Courageous* reminded me of what we mean to each other. It turns out that going down sucks at the time, but finding yourself in a new life is the best. The remainder of this book is how I found my new life, and how you can find yours in your divorce situation.

Turning Lemons into Lemonade

We all go through struggles during divorce, but you can turn your struggles into blessings. Life is what you focus on! You can choose to be happy, or you can choose to be unhappy. Your divorce process is a negative, disappointing, and emotional process. You have the power to choose how you will fight the battle. Will you remain positive and optimistic, or will you be negative and cause everyone around you to run for cover?

Over the years of attending Doorkeepers, I continued to grow into a man who I could be proud of. My whole life began to change. I was transforming into a person with a serving heart. Love your neighbor as thyself took on a whole new meaning. When your family does not recognize you anymore, in many cases (and certainly in mine), that's a good thing. I stopped watching the news; I started listening to healthy and positive books in my car. The transformation wasn't just with my relationships; it was at the very core of my being. I felt like my soul had been transformed, allowing me to live and love on a higher level than I had ever experienced.

Fill out the following questions, be as specific as possible. (Use extra paper if necessary.)

1. Is there a time in your life when you admitted defeat?

2. How did that make you feel, deep inside?

3. What was that like to go through?

4. Looking back on the experiences of your life, are you still holding onto anything that is weighing you down?

5. Do you have a support system in your life to help you with this?

Chapter Six
Finding Blessings in Unusual Places

Let me backtrack just a bit. I told you about the financial wreckage my poor judgment had caused to our bank accounts. But I didn't really share with you the damage that was done to my marriage. Our marriage barely survived an almost certain divorce. I was looking for a way out, a way to stop the pain and end the misery. It wasn't fair to my wife, and I felt it would be better if we divorced. So, I demanded a divorce and accepted full responsibility for the mess we were in.

My wife never gave up. That's one of the perks of marrying a strong woman. I could feel God changing my heart. My wife suddenly suggested we attend a different church. I was not open to the idea at all, but then for some reason, I decided to try it out. Now that I look back on it, there isn't one thing that I can say changed my *very certain mind*; but two things I know for sure, it was God's grace and a stubborn wife!

Rearview Blessings

Life is strange, isn't it? I've learned a lot in my crazy up-and-down journey of life. One thing I've learned for sure; with some blessings, you only see them in the rearview mirror. In 2009, while putting our marriage back together, my wife took a trip to Florida to see her parents. She called me in tears. She said the doctor told her that if she did not take care of her parents, he would have to call in adult services. That totally blindsided us. We were expecting her to go down and visit with her parents for a while, and instead, she was plunged into making a major life-changing decision on behalf of her parents. We were able to calm the tears and fears. Together, we hatched a plan to get them to Michigan.

Her dad was convinced after much persuasion, so now I know where my wife gets her stubbornness! However, her mother, who had dementia, started throwing cherry tomatoes at my wife as an expression of her revolt. She refused to leave her home. We made arrangements and concocted a plan to fly out to Florida and bring them both back.

One week before the move, my father-in-law called; his wife was hospitalized with mini-strokes. She would never regain her mind. My wife went down because she had to be with her parents at once. A decision was made that my wife would help her father load up a trailer to move him to Michigan. We later kidnapped her mother out of the hospital, made possible because her sister was a nurse. The hospital was willing to sign over my mother-in-law's care to a registered nurse.

We drove all night, stopping only for gas, and checked her into the West Bloomfield Nursing Home. My wife used her skill to find a facility with an independent living center and a nursing home. My in-laws were safe and within the same facility. It was a stressful and hard time in our lives. Remember, we were still trying to heal our almost destroyed marriage.

More Life Changes

My mother-in-law passed on a few years after we relocated her and my father-in-law to Michigan. After the loss of his lifelong partner, my father-in-law felt like he wanted a place he could call his own, to have some time to reconfigure his new life. We set off to look for a place he could call his own.

For the next several weeks, our weekends were spent with a realtor, looking for a suitable place. We'd eventually found a HUD condo that needed some tender loving care. I grabbed a few friends and recruited the needed help, and my father-in-law's place was born. He lived just down the street from my wife and me, and it was perfect for him. At this time, as if we didn't have enough going on, my wife separated from her almost thirty-year career, and we decided to let go of our family home. (We never did like to get bored!) It was a hard decision; we had the home built when the children were firstborn, and of course, it was chock-full of great memories. But we were committed to living within our means.

A Gift from God

On Friday, while looking for property near her father's house, we found a property with an in-law suite. Her dad exclaimed, "I could live there." My wife responded, "Dad would you really like to live with us?" He responded without hesitation, "That would be great." My wife had received a severance package, and I agreed to sell my beautiful Ford F-250 diesel truck. Her dad committed to selling the condo. That Sunday after church, we went on a mission. We must have driven by 30 homes that day, but it was the last home that makes this story so remarkable. We went back to the neighborhood, dreaming one day of having a home like that. "That's it!"

my wife exclaimed. It was a beautiful home, and we called right away.

The realtor answered our call. The house had just gone on the market that day, and we were the fourth to view it. She said, "See you at 4." We quickly snatched Dad, and within moments we were inspecting our new home. It was perfect! There was a main floor master and bath for Dad, and three bedrooms upstairs for my wife, our teenage boys, and me. The downstairs basement was spacious and finished and was a perfect place for our boys to have company. The great room had a vaulted ceiling and a natural fireplace, which we all loved, especially Dad.

We knew we had to act fast because others were interested. I called a friend of mine from Bible study, who was a realtor. He came at night, and we spent until after 11 p.m. preparing our offer. Our realtor presented the offer on Monday. By Thursday, it was unclear as to whether or not we would be selected. We had offered more than their asking price, but I knew that wasn't enough.

In God's wisdom, I felt strongly that the house would appraise lower than our offer, and it would be of great appeal to the seller if our bid was not contingent on the appraisal. I called the realtor to request the change. He explained all the reasons why I shouldn't do it, but I demanded the change. It worked! We bought the property, and that is how we ended up in our perfect home.

Living with Dad

Like everybody these days, I tend to have as many plates to juggle as possible. We got moved in with Dad. When you join three generations of family under the same roof, magic does happen, but maybe not right away. That first year was full of compromise. There was a lot of love and tolerance. Looking back in my life, I realize that the most difficult times are the times that made me a better person.

It's funny, but when I was in school, I remember how much I hated those teachers who pushed me and forced me to achieve my full potential. Today, those are the teachers I recognize with honor. Those times that I spent with Dad, although I did not know it at the time, were the best times. During this time, Dad got to really know his grandchildren, and they really got to know and love him too. I watched as Dad renewed his relationship with his daughter in a deeper and more loving way. Dad and I were as thick as thieves.

I remember when he first moved in, and we relocated his 55-gallon fish tank to the center wall of our living room. When I came home, he and my wife had plotted for a 100-gallon tank. I had to think fast that day as I suggested putting the tank in the wall. The discussion resulted in a 170-gallon tank and a turtle tank in our foyer. The completed tank was gorgeous, and the first thing commented on by all who entered.

Dad passed in 2018, but the memories we shared live on. Never in my life would I have had a fish tank, much less one of size and beauty. The fish are so beautiful, and I see them every day, which reminds me of him. There was a time when we caught him with potting soil in the bathroom. We knew he couldn't go outside, exclaiming, "Dad, you're not going to plant flowers in this tub!" He said, "No!" The proof was right in front of us—the flowers in the tub. There was one time when we went all the way to the east side of town to get barstools that fit him perfectly. All of the adventures we had in going to the cider mill, to Florida, on camping trips, there are so many memories that influence the way I live my life.

During our time together, Dad's health continued to fail. One of the first things I remember is convincing him he no longer needed a car. Our youngest had just turned sixteen, and I persuaded dad to give up his car to his grandson. I thought I was so smart until I discovered that he had purchased a new car. It was always something.

I remember when he felt he couldn't stand up alone in his shower. This required immediate action. My wife and I found a walk-in tub on Marketplace; when we brought it home, we recruited assistance to install it. The tub didn't fit, and I was up all night trying to figure out how it would work. I told my friend that we could cut the fiberglass and it would fit. My friend laughed, but it worked. Towards the end of his life, he went blind and needed 24-hour care. He demanded that my wife get him a bell. I think she thought he was kidding, but we all took him seriously when he refused to eat until we got him a bell. I went online and found him a smaller bell that he could hold on to, and a bigger ship-like bell we mounted by his bed. At his memorial service, we celebrated Dad's life by ringing the bell to honor him.

Fill out the following questions, be as specific as possible. (Use extra paper if necessary.)

1. What have you experienced in your life that you absolutely did not want to do? But, when you did it, the experience changed your life forever.

2. Write out what that experience meant to you and why it meant so much?

3. Please list how it changed your life.

Chapter Seven
So Long, Self

Jesus talked about a grain of wheat. If the grain stays of itself, it remains only a single kernel; however, if the kernel of grain dies and goes to the ground, it will become a great harvest. That Scripture really touched my heart. Whether we accept it or not, we all are dying to self or holding on to our single life. I have accepted this wisdom as true. Dying to myself has become a daily prayer for me. I want to be a new creation. I want to be that person who serves, who loves generously, who forgives immediately, and who is a person of his word. I know I do not do this perfectly, but I make it a living priority to practice every day. Paul, in Galatians, says we need to be fruit inspectors. If we are patient, loving, kind, merciful, not vengeful, if we are not boastful or puffed up, then we are humble servants.

That was a life-changing time for me. I was not only transformed on the outside; I was made new from the inside out. In my email, it does not say 'attorney at law,' it now says 'humble servant.' I do this not to tell others who I am but to remind myself. That reminds me of a story. When you first learn to ride a bike, balance is important. One of the ways I have learned whether I am a true person to my new life is in traffic when I am tense. It's so easy to get agitated and upset with everyone on the road. It's in moments like that I have learned to recognize that I am not that person with the good fruit.

Some may say, "If you are the courteous driver, you will never get ahead." What I have found is this: It takes more energy, causes more time delays, and gets in the way (more often than not) from living a productive life. What bothers me, if I let it, is that I cannot stand people getting ahead of me. Challenge your thinking. Do you like the world the way it is? I've heard it said that we are not to conform to the patterns of this world. (These may be strange words to you; they were for me.) The words are followed by, "be transformed" and then the how—" by a renewing of your mind" to think differently.

These words truly caused a transformation in me. As I have lived my new life in the context of how I used to live, I knew I needed a new way of thinking. Every day became a new discovery. Someone once told me that every human being, at their core, does two things. I confirmed "only" two things? Yes, your entire life is lived by making yourself look good or avoiding looking bad. True, isn't it?

You can work around that by becoming conscious of your behavior. Based on my goals and desires, I am conscious of my behavior. I want to be selfless, humble, and service-oriented. There are so many distractions, and the gravity of life pulls us to self-centered behavior so easily. Therefore, I must be intentional in allowing the new life I want and continue to grow so I can defeat the self-centered desires.

Fill out the following questions, be as specific as possible. (Use extra paper if necessary.)

1. Do you think there are a right way and a wrong way to think about a problem?

2. If you're facing divorce, please list the right ways to approach the divorce.

3. List the wrong ways to approach your divorce.

Chapter Eight
Divorce Done the Right Way

At this point, some of you are saying, "Tim, this is great for you, and I enjoyed learning about your transformation, but how does this help me? I am in (or heading into) a wicked divorce!"

This is what I know: Most of you are approaching your circumstances in the wrong way, from a self-centered way. To say it another way, you are looking at yourself as a victim, or defensive, or prideful, or other emotions easy to detect for anyone else. Consider my "true confession" as to my old way of being, that I cared more about myself than my client.

My clients needed me most when I focused on their anger, bitterness, and rage within them. I believed I was serving their best interests by giving them what they wanted. This also benefited me financially. Clients wanted me to fight for them, to take their side and agree with them, no matter how ridiculous. The expected response was always to fight in court. I loved to demonstrate my litigation skills and earn a big payday. How do I sum up my "old way" of being? I took advantage of my clients' vulnerabilities. My honest question to you is this: Is there a better way? Do you want to learn a better way?

This is Another Way to Consider Your Answers

Will I fall prey to an alligator lawyer? You are guaranteed to fall prey to this type of attorney if you hire an attorney who tells you ONLY what you want to hear. Think about playing poker. Do you think the winning hand always wins? That sounds silly, right? It's not true; in fact, many times, the winning hand ends up losing. What is the key? That's right: EMOTION!

Think of hiring a lawyer as a poker game. You have cards; they're your emotions, and your attorney is dealt with some emotions as well. Who is in control? Of course, the attorney, but why? He is in better control of his emotions. If you present your hand (as is often the case) due to a full range of emotions that are common to divorce, you will be out of control. If your emotions were your cards, you would be literally showing the other players (prospective lawyers) the cards in your hand. Do you think the other players will let you know they can see your cards? HECK NO!

Even worse, we justify the loss at the table (behavior) because we are angry and find others to blame. At this point, you may be thinking, "How does he know," or worse, you're saying, "That's not me!" Remember, this is *Confessions of a Divorce Lawyer*. There are two things I need you to be very clear about. If you cannot reach a conscious state of understanding with yourself and you are vulnerable in your current emotional state, then you are more likely to be that person I talk to in a social setting after your divorce. You are telling me all about the spouse, the attorney, the court system, and the Friend of the Court (FOC) referee who ruined your life. Here's the really sad part. If you think it's hard going through the divorce, then listen to this next part very carefully. When I ask how long they have been divorced, many times, the answer is "over 20 years." Brothers and sisters, I understand, but I am here to convince you: that person does not have to be you.

Don't Fall Prey to Hungry Attorneys

What does the culture tell us? Friends, family, advertisements, and often attorneys will tell you that you need to "WIN." The world and your desires tell you to "get what you deserve."

This, of course, creates a battlefield arena, and no one wins. You don't win, and your children, your friends who constantly hear and feel your anger and bitterness, don't win.

There is Someone Who Does Win — the Attorney.

The attorney has built up a healthy bill as the battle rages. The attorney that once appeared as the only person on your side is now revealed as the person who was only interested in your money. It is not the fault of that attorney; it is your fault for agreeing to pay someone to tell you what you wanted to hear. It is the old adage; two attorneys walk into a bar, and the bartender tells them he was looking for a divorce attorney. The first attorney says, "I am the best attorney in town and will win for you everything you want." The other attorney tells him, "The process is nasty, and you have to consider all of the circumstances," and these are his only assurances. "I will be with you to help and guide you to make the right decisions so that you will start your new life right." Okay, the adage may not be old, and it may not even be an adage, but work with me. 😉

We only need to turn to the advertising offered by divorce attorneys to realize which attorney most will select. This reveals to me why I spent most of my time advertising www.toughlitigator.com - a lawyer who wins!

My slogan was "Hire A Lawyer With A Bite." All my marketing material reflected this message. I advertised it on my cars and proudly displayed it everywhere. For Christmas, the family knew they could get me a gift with a gator.

BITE!

HIRE A
LAWYER
WITH
BITE!
888-89-GATOR
TOUGHLITIGATOR.COM

Select the Right Attorney

If I have not given you pause to think already, I want to give you a couple more things to think about. Attorneys tend to intimidate and make those *uneducated in the law* feel inferior. Let's face it; the fact is that everybody is uneducated in the law, except the attorney. When an attorney does this to you, it embarrasses and shames you into not asking questions. This prevents you from asking important questions you need to know when hiring an attorney. I hesitate to provide you a list in the fear that you may consider it as exhaustive. There is no way I can do that, but these are **some** of the questions you should take with you to an interview and ask:

1. How do you propose to know about me during the case, and is that important?

2. How do you propose to know about my spouse, and is that important?

3. How do you propose to get information about the case, such as assets and debts, and information about the children?

4. Do you believe we should first find out areas of common ground, before discussing disputes?

5. Would you find it helpful if I have a list of facts containing what my spouse agrees with and a list of disputed issues?

6. Do you advocate that I remain a loving person even when I am mad at my spouse and want to go to court and fight?

7. Will you remind me of my need to remain loving even when I do not want to?

8. Do you advocate that I forgive my spouse, even when I do not think my spouse is worthy of forgiveness?

9. Will you remind me of my need to forgive, even when I do not want to?

10. What are your thoughts regarding integrity? Give me some examples of how you have implemented integrity in your life.

Divorce Workshop

In 2016, I formed a group that I called *Divorce Workshop*. I recruited a dozen people who were as passionate as I was to improve the divorce process. Each party had themselves been divorced. We met once a month for a period of six months. It was not difficult to have meaningful discussions surrounding this topic, but none of the discussions were without raw emotion. This shocked me, given most of them were divorced over a decade ago. I did not expect the pain I felt.

The best way I can describe my pain is to utilize a storyline from the movie *Something's Gotta Give,* starring Jack Nicholson and Diane Keaton. Nicholson plays a wealthy playboy who falls in love with Keaton. This is the first falling-in-love experience for Nicholson. Keaton forces a relationship that Nicholson is not prepared to accept. He quickly finds out the pain love can cause, and he goes off on an escapade to determine how each woman in all his former relationships felt about him. The movie depicts various negative actions, including shutting the door in his face, calling him bad names, and worse. One woman took the time to tell him straight up what she felt about him. Of course, this was a painful educational process, as was the divorce workshop for me.

When it came to discussing their divorce, what I saw was a group of people wounded with regrets, hatred, unforgivingness, and a loss of their identity. I'll never forget the third time we met when I had asked what could be done differently to help people deal with their divorce. One of the parties stated, "what I needed was hope." The process changed the way I see a person going through a divorce process, and how I see my role in representing a party in a divorce. The divorce workshop was a success in assisting me in my role as an attorney; however, I believed it would destroy me financially. What emerged was a new way of being for those in a state of divorce with love, forgiveness, and integrity.

Building a Strong Foundation

Let me tell you a story. When we were building our house back in 1996, we went to visit the home every Sunday. We were so excited, anticipating the ability to move in and start our lives. We were at the house when the footings went in, and the basement was poured. I could not believe how many footings there were and how deep they went. I had a chance to talk to one of the workers who was taking a coffee break. He told me that if they did not get this stage of the construction right, nothing else mattered. It didn't mean much then, but as I read the Bible and Jesus telling us about a wrong foundation built on sand—it does not hold when troubles come. However, a strong foundation build on the rock can withstand all your troubles. A strong foundation includes love, forgiveness, and integrity.

Take your life to a new beginning. Be generous. Grow in hope. Have a servant's heart. Think greater than yourself. Be an example for your children, your family, and your sphere of influence. Does that sound impossible in your situation right now? We all have a sphere of influence. The way to get through the toughest times is to get your eyes off yourself and focus on others—your kids, your new life—whatever is important to you. Think of it as letting yourself build a new and strong foundation for your future life.

Maybe your new life plan includes a new home, a proper budget, or happy children. All of these things add up to a life worth living. How good would it feel to hear others say, "You inspire me by the way you are handling your divorce." Be a motivation for your friends and family, be inspired by and for your children, love greatly, forgive unnaturally, and remain true to your word. During a divorce, a lot of decisions must be made. They are tough decisions. They are usually painful as well. Make sure the tough decisions become the right decisions. Remember, you will go on to live a full life after the divorce. It matters how people remember your behavior during a divorce. Impress people with your character and honesty. My hope is that you will not fall prey to the wrong attorney.

Character Matters

Integrity matters when people, and even attorneys, are cheering you on to "Fight, Fight, Fight." You don't have to go down that road. Remember, everything that you say will have an impact and influence on your children, but the influence doesn't stop with your children. Do you want it to be a positive influence or a negative influence? You will have to go on to live your life with your family, your work associates, your friends, and even your enemies. Remember that the harder you work to transform yourself, the greater will be the results in your life, and the greater the influence will be on the people you care about the most.

My greatest encouragement to my clients is to allow others to show their toxic behavior. There are always plenty of examples out there to see who aren't able to listen to this advice and end up more miserable after the divorce than they were before. Early on in my love, forgiveness, and integrity transition, I had a client who was bruised badly and stuck in hate and unforgivingness. I cannot blame this type of emotion when the spouse was physically abusive. I showed love and modeled forgiveness while remaining in my integrity. There were many occasions where I wanted to act differently.

I recall a FOC hearing where my client refused to answer questions. I requested a recess and informed my client of the need to cooperate. She was belligerent, angry, and disrespectful. I responded in kind, getting in her face with anger and a threatening tone. This did nothing to change her behavior.

The next time we were in court, this client brought her mother. As I discussed the client's case with the mother present, her mother stated, "Is this where you are going to threaten my daughter as you did before?" I had nothing to say. That was a Friday. I knew what I had to do, and I knew why I had to do it, but as God is my witness, I didn't want to do it. That is why I did it. I called that client on a Saturday, and I asked for forgiveness for over an hour. When I was done with the phone call, I felt like I settled a million-dollar case.

What did I learn from my experience? I learned that love, forgiveness, and integrity start with me. Too often in my career, I, unbeknownst to myself, lived in hate, unforgivingness, and poor character. This negatively affected my emotions and impacted every relationship, especially those closest to me, my wife, and children. I am concerned about the client's wellbeing as she proceeds forward. Despite my resounding influence and advocacy towards love and forgiveness, my client continued her course. However, if I were to see her again, I would remain in love.

Your Thoughts and Words Matter

"Your thoughts and words matter." I can't say that too many times when I am working with clients. Many people go through life without ever thinking about their daily thoughts. One of the biggest eye-openers for me is found in Joel Osteen's book *Your Best Life Now*, and its discussions about thoughts and words. It inspired me to inventory my thoughts daily. I thought I was a positive and uplifting person, but I had to admit that many of my thoughts were negative and toxic. Becoming conscious of negative or toxic areas in your life is powerful.

You must become intentional about becoming conscious of negative thoughts and words in your life every day.

Words matter!

- What are you saying?
- Who are you saying it to?
- Who are your friends?
- Are your friends inspiring you to be the best version of yourself, or are they bringing you down?
- What TV shows are you watching or binging?
- What are you listening to in the car?

- What other forms of entertainment do you gravitate towards?
- Do you feel you have to change?

So what did my Divorce Workshop do to help those going through a divorce? I learned that the way to go through a divorce is with love and forgiveness! Don't leave me now! Discover and experience how your difficult and painful divorce struggle can blossom into a beautiful new life. Let me encourage you to have hope.

The Right Way Versus the Wrong Way

There is a right way and a wrong way to go through your divorce, so be on the right side. Focus on the people you hold dear to you. Your decision-making should be after you cool off and can be forgiving, and when you can emotionally make a well-thought-out decision. Have an inner circle of people you trust to go to about your decision-making, not your problems. Your friends should not be recruited because they will take your side. Those friends in all likelihood are using you for their benefit.

Fill out the following questions, be as specific as possible. (Use extra paper if necessary.)

1. What kind of divorce do you desire for yourself, your children, and your family?

2. What are you willing to do to make sure that desire is fulfilled?

3. Take an inventory of your thoughts, words, friends, activities, what you listen to, and why?

4. Are you willing to change them?

5. What could you do to replace negative activities?

Chapter Nine
So Your Spouse Isn't Playing Fair

How's That Work?

In my old way of being, I thought more of myself and what I wanted out of the client relationship. This would naturally put me into a position of needing my client to win—my client must win, the spouse must lose, for me to feel important. This naturally resulted in me assuming the emotions of my clients. Finding love, forgiveness, and integrity created a new way of being for me. When faced with difficult emotional situations, I learned to pause and collect myself.

To help you understand the importance of this discovery, think about the last time you were engaged in a highly emotional conversation. You make a statement you regret. If you could go back in time and reassess the conversation, can you visualize the conversation ending differently? Of course, you can. The reason you can is that your emotions have receded. This allows you to remain objective during times when you otherwise would not.

Love, forgiveness, and integrity are emotions found deep within a person that is like a lost treasure leading to great power and wisdom. Power comes from within.

The Gator, Only Better

All those years of being an aggressive advocator were not lost! The need to advocate for my client is always present. Knowing what you are doing, how to conduct discovery, when to conduct depositions, and the need for trial skills is worth its weight in gold when hiring your attorney. The many skills I developed over the years are far superior when I act with love, forgiveness, and integrity, and when I remain objective and place my client's interest at the center of the discussion. Remaining strong while keeping my emotions in check offers the right solution in a highly emotional situation. What I have learned is that my ability to remain calm and objective provides the assurances my clients deserve.

I recently handled a case for a client, suggesting their spouse come in to discuss the "one attorney" divorce process. We had proceeded through three long meetings when a breakdown occurred. The spouse hired an attorney, and the case was resolved through the mediation process. I received a call a few months later from my client, stating there was a lawsuit filed before the divorce proceeding. I filed a motion-based upon failure to disclose the asset, and in the response were allegations that the asset was disclosed during our private meetings, which were recorded—who does that! I received a fancy subpoena to testify and disclose my file. At the hearing, the Judge shined favor upon my client, and we were victorious.

The case, as they all do in one way or another, tested my emotions. I was so mad that this person would record settlement meetings in such a devious way. I know there are times when we all feel betrayed. In this situation, it was very personal; my ability to remain in love, forgiveness, and integrity was put to the test. I came through the experience of feeling proud. I did not let my emotions get the better of me, so instead, I was victorious in so many ways. I did learn from the experience and have since revised my "One Attorney Agreement" to include, no recording of any kind.

Do You Really Think the Fight is Over Stuff?

In one case, a couple was ready to go to trial over a painting they both wanted. In exploring their respective desires, it turned out the painting was purchased on their honeymoon. It represented the best time of their short-term relationship, and (here's the funny part) was *titled The Joy of Love*. I know the Judge would have made a quick decision: "Sell the painting and split the difference." But the other attorney and I decided to use this moment to teach our clients about what is important in life. I honestly do not remember who was awarded the painting, but I do recall that in the end, each party learned a great deal about hidden emotions.

More and more in my new way of being, I have noticed that the stuff you say you want isn't what you really want. The stuff is just the shield protecting you from a broken heart. What you are guarding is the hurt, the betrayal, and all the other emotions. I recently had someone tell me that when it comes to suffering, people will do anything to avoid it. I was told the truth, that it's better to go right through the suffering; it makes us stronger, less vulnerable, and less exploitable—or maybe it's better said that taking on suffering provides a better foundation.

I love *My Cousin Vinny*. In the movie, Vinny is questioning his fiancé about the differences between positraction and limited-slip traction. She answers the difference by explaining, "If you ever got stuck in the mud in Alabama, you would know the difference." In other words, limited-slip is when only one tire spins, and then it keeps digging further and further into the mud. On many occasions, people get stuck, like the one-wheel spinning, going deeper and deeper into your problems. Don't get stuck and stay stuck, use positraction (your new way of being) to forge a new path (your new life) for YOU.

Blind Spots in Your Life Can Cause Continued Damage

Newer cars come with built-in alarms to tell us when another driver is in our blind spot. If only people were equipped with sensors to inform us of our emotional blind spots. In life are those circumstantial things we know—because of how we were raised, where we went to school and our surroundings. There are also things we know that we do not know. I know I can't fly a plane! But if I were to draw a circle and draw in two pieces of the pie, that would include all you know or don't know. The 80% remainder of the circle would include the information you don't even know that you don't know. I have made it a mission in my life to identify in me those things I don't know, my blind spots. Blind spots have to be revealed to you through experience leading to consciousness. They are often seen by others, but you cannot see them.

I represented a client who could only see things one way. He wanted to give his wife everything and be left alone. He could not say that running from his suffering would not settle the matter. He reached a different level of understanding when she called the police on him, and he ended up in a hotel with a Personal Protection Order filed against him. He called me, and I met him at the hotel. There were several blind spots revealed that day. As I showed a broken person love, he began seeing his situation differently. His wife had a pit bull of an attorney, but I kept showing and encouraging love, forgiving him, and being my word. My client witnessed the power as he desired a different approach. The good thing was that he trusted me, and I inspired him in greater ways. My client was willing to walk away from everything but ended up with over $200,000 in assets. As they say on the *A-Team,* "I love it when a plan comes together."

The Right Attorney

How do you know if you have the right attorney? Your attorney should advocate for the right reasons, not just your reasons. Your lawyer should discuss things fully with you, not in legal terms, but in terms you understand. The lawyer should not intimidate you or make you afraid to ask anything. You need to know, to trust down deep, that your attorney is 100% for you during a difficult and emotional time. You should have no doubt in your mind, knowing that your lawyer is not taking advantage of your vulnerabilities but embracing them. Your attorney should be willing to discuss the importance of love, forgiveness, and integrity to your case because they inspire others to do what is best. Everyone is a winner when both parties are committed to making the divorce work.

Fill out the following questions, be as specific as possible. (Use extra paper if necessary.)

1. How do you think your spouse will respond to the divorce?

2. Are you open to love, forgiveness, and integrity in your divorce process?

3. What kind of attorney are you looking for, and why?

Chapter Ten
Go the Distance

At the start of my transformation, I became fixated on the movie *Field of Dreams.* Kevin Costner, the star, plays a farmer who is hearing voices. (If you have not seen the movie, this may not mean as much to you.) The movie gave Costner's character a series of tests that transformed his life in the end. A scene that always draws me in is when he takes Terence Mann to a baseball game. They both get a message, "go the distance" but only Costner accepts the message—at first. That describes a lot of us; we hear the message, but we refuse, we resist, we're living in fear, we feel like "it's too good to be true," and on and on it goes. Mr. Mann, fighting his own demons, becomes more open to change when he admits to Costner that he heard the voice too. When I think back over my life, how many voices have I missed? How many chances did I have to turn my life around?

If you are reading this book and thinking about divorce, you are hearing a voice saying, "Go the distance!"

Transforming Your Life: My Go the Distance Transformation.

So I married in 1981 and divorced in 1983. Does anyone want to guess how long I remained buried in my hurts? This is the saddest part. Not until *2016* was I finally able to let go of my hurts, pains, regrets, and (most of all) my feelings of rejection. Early on in my practice, I carried around these failures that fueled my representation of others who had similar hurts. I wish I could go back and change the past, but I must let it go. I was forced to face many blind spots in my life. The constant pressure to change was with me, and all of the proper influences in my life that pushed me over the finish line to true freedom. My transformation journey brought me to a point where I could no longer deny that I had buried my responsibility in the broken marriage from so many years ago. Let me encourage you: Go the Distance!

The Hardest Call I'd Ever Make Or So I Thought!

In 2016, I mustered the courage to walk through my fear, shame, anger, and rage and called my ex-wife. For the next 45 minutes, I asked for forgiveness; I identified the things I did wrong, and I explained to her all the ways in which I had blamed her, and how that was wrong. This was a funny thing, and I know some of you will enjoy this during the 45 minutes I poured out my heart and soul, not once did she say or admit to doing anything wrong. Isn't that how it usually works?

It did not matter to me; I was free. But it was revealed, that in the face of an opportunity to take responsibility and approach her demons, she decided it was better to keep those demons to herself. Do not be the norm. Push through your pride and allow transformation to set you free. My new way of being was just put into practice.

I had just put the finishing touches on our love, forgiveness, and integrity website (www.AshandAsh.org) and gave the green light to publish when I received a call. The individual set an appointment, and we met.

At first, this person wanted to see if I was for real, that I stood for what was written on the website. This person studied the website very carefully, pointing out a couple of typos. In the next hour and a half, the person's skeptical nature was challenged. He stated that he did not believe the process as possible, but he would consider it.

In the following week, this person called for a follow-up meeting; again, we met, and I described the process and answered questions. To my surprise, the person retained me. The divorce process encountered many emotional moments as they always do, and the person was amazed at the effectiveness of the process in assisting with controlling emotion, improving prospective, and improving decision-making ability. Can I say this person received more of the assets or otherwise won? No, I cannot. What I can say is that the person received a reasonable settlement and came complete with his divorce. This person raves, not about me, but about the process. (Oh, this person loves me too.) 😊

It is my hope and prayer for those faced with a divorce that you will also become complete with your divorce, as did the above client.

Fill out the following questions, be as specific as possible. (Use extra paper if necessary.)

1. What are my blind spots?

2. Do I consider others when I think about my divorce?

3. How often do I consider the thoughts, desires, and emotions of others?

4. Am I behaving in a way I'm proud of?

5. Am I modeling behavior that I want to be remembered for?

Chapter Eleven
My Advice to You

As I pen these words, admittedly, I am in the second year of advocating for love, forgiveness, and integrity as a divorce attorney. When I say advocate, I start with myself, then my client, the opposing side, the FOC, the Judge, and with a bullhorn out to all who will listen. In less than two years, the challenges to bring the possibility of love, forgiveness, and integrity have been fraught with many fears, a huge amount of anxiety and one death (myself); no tears were shed, only love, joy, and happiness. My wife says she even likes me better too!

I will not speak for those clients who I represented, but I will share one very cool moment. The case was before the court with hopes for a resolution. The main stumbling block was an affair by one of the parties. These difficulties are sometimes hard to resolve. The dominating emotion is quite often HATE! Both parties were committed to an amicable resolution, and in fact, one was reached. The court clerk took us back to the jury room, where we reduced the settlement to writing. As the parties signed the document, I stated, "We need to do one more thing. I looked at my client and asked this party to look into the eyes of the other party and ask for forgiveness." They did. I then did the same thing with the other party, directed to my client. When walking away, I do not know about the feelings of my client, the opposing counsel, the opposing party, or the court—but I felt like I was walking on water.

Have the Proper Vision

When you are heading into a divorce, it is so important to have a vision that's flexible and accommodating. The vision you have must go beyond you. If you have been raising the kids and your spouse is leaving you, it can be debilitating. Gaining a vision may be the hardest thing you do. The vision is different for everyone and is always ever-expanding. For the person above, there is a new career on the horizon, possibly a new home, and so many other changes. This may cause so much anxiety and fear that it is difficult to get started.

I heard it said that if your business is down, help someone else with their business. This principle has proven beneficial for me, time, and time again. The same can be true for you! If you are having trouble creating a vision for your new life, then look to the others who will be affected by your changes. The most obvious will be your children, if applicable. However, everyone has someone in their life that will be greatly affected by your divorce. Go beyond yourself to a vision for your life that includes those who are supportive of you.

Create a Circle of Trust

The hit comedy, *Meet the Fockers*, starred Robert DeNiro as a protective dad who invented a "circle of trust." I recommend this example—you need a circle of trust. I call it my inner circle. This is a group of people who you can trust, no matter what. These people care for you more than just telling you what you want to hear. CAUTION: If you are a person who never wants to hear anyone else's opinion, you are most certainly at a significant risk of being exploited and disappointed with how your divorce will turn out.

Your circle of trust should include your attorney, counselor (if you have one), spiritual advisor (if you have one), trusted friend(s) whose opinion you value, employee, or employer. Can you think of any others?

Wisdom Leads to Better Decisions

When executed, the proper vision provides a solid foundation. The proper foundation prepares you for the *"what ifs"* of life. As an example, if your financial budget includes a property that requires every dollar to pay all your bills, this provides an unstable foundation. One unexpected repair on the car and your foundation get washed away. We must expect the unexpected and plan for troubles.

It seems so difficult at first, but fighting off the urge to get things done, or having things resolved so we can get back to normal, is the culture's way of creating anxiety and fear in your life. Don't jump at the first plan, or the second, or third; keep searching until you are confident that the foundation is sturdy and true, able to withstand the troubles of life.

Continue to Hold on to Hope

Some people are natural optimists; they always see the glass as half-full. I am one of them. Whatever happens, I am always thinking that this is going to end up in my favor. Some of you are cursing me right now, and some are saying, "Why can't that be me?" The truth is—I don't know! Why does hope come more naturally to some than to others? Everybody has their own cross to carry.

What I do know is that whether the feelings and emotions of hope come more naturally, or they are difficult to experience, you must continue to have hope, experience hope, and put hope at the forefront of your mind. Hope is essential to your divorce process. If it helps you to think you have to do it for your kids, your family, your friends, people at work—JUST DO IT.

Suffering is Required

So many people going through the divorce process do everything they can to avoid suffering. Sadly, some people even think that if they pay their attorney enough money, they can buy their way out of suffering. They get criminal law confused with family law. In criminal law, you can arguably hire the right attorney who will get your charges removed. The same is not true for divorce. In a divorce, either one side or the other, or both sides have decided to go their separate way(s). Just in considering the financial devastation of separation and the division of income you will suffer, this fact alone is insignificant next to the pain and suffering caused to the human emotions.

Don't cover up your emotions, embrace them! This statement might seem odd, but the more you suffer through your divorce process, the healthier you will be at its conclusion. I am constantly pressing upon my clients to push through difficult decisions, difficult emotions, and suffering in general. When you refuse to deal with suffering, but avoid problems instead, you are giving in to the actions that will leave you open to be victimized by a greedy attorney. I don't know how many clients who have sought my services after their divorce attorney failed to resolve their case on key and difficult issues. These clients experience a second divorce process. The good news is that these people are open to my counsel. However, I want you to be prepared for the first time!

Fill out the following questions, be as specific as possible. (Use extra paper if necessary.)

1. Would you rather have an attorney who encourages love or hate?

2. What is your position on forgiveness?

3. When you fail to keep your word, how does that make you feel?

Chapter Twelve
This Could Change the World

There is so much hatred in the world. Divorce statistics are staggering. Over 50% of marriages end in divorce. How many of those end in hatred, no forgiveness, and moral decay? The stark reality is that the ripple effect of divorce is felt on the family generationally. How many children or grandchildren are products of divorce? You get the picture. Our society has created generational poverty. I must take ownership of my role in this problem. For nearly two decades, I moved, touched, and inspired people towards hate, vengeance, and doing whatever it takes to WIN.

I boast freely of my transformation. I am unashamed of my belief in Jesus Christ. I have investigated the rearview mirror of my life. I have suffered, felt tremendous fear and anxiety, stepped out of my comfort zone, and experienced great sorrow. However, as Scripture says (it is God's ever presence in my life), joy came in the morning. My transformation continues, and my confessions in this book are both frightening and beautiful. I have experienced "dark nights of the soul" moments impacting my ego, identity, and pride. My nature is to protect ME, and I sought to defend my independence through control, power, and defensive actions. When I became conscious of these actions and saw them as destructive of ME, of those I loved, and the world as a whole, then true transformation became possible.

Now I see a beautiful world full of renewal and redemption. Love, forgiveness, and integrity can cause even the broken relationship to transform. Children who see parents love, rather than hate, will be transformed. Children that see forgiveness, when vengeance appears to be the right course, will be transformed into a world of forgiveness. Children who see parents sticking with doing what they said they would, even when it hurts, will be transformed into people of character and integrity. As we face a divorce, we often do not consider the destruction of our self-centered decisions. This is why I stand for divorce with LOVE rather than making decisions that have life-altering effects. I stand for divorce with FORGIVENESS as opposed to holding onto bitterness, anger, and a need to get back for the betrayals. I want you to maintain your character and integrity, even when everyone in the culture is telling you something different. I stand for these things because I know it will change the world.

Fill out the following questions, be as specific as possible. (Use extra paper if necessary.)

1. Can the way you handle your divorce change the world?

2. How important is it to you to stand for something in your divorce?

Chapter Thirteen
It's Worth It!

It would take an entire book to discuss the toxic relationship I created with my son during law school, and how the early years of my practicing law negatively impacted our relationship. There are too many regrets for me to discuss. However, today is like a rainbow; the clouds are gone, and the sun has revealed itself. There was a time when all three of my children hated me and avoided me. I can't express how that made me feel because I just didn't care. I was too busy building my empire.

I remember that I would come home late at night to discover the kids' toys in the driveway. I would have to get out of my car after a long day of dealing with angry clients and move the toys so I could put my car in the garage. When I came into the house, I would attack the whole family, destroying my ability to have any relationship with them. This is but one example of many over the course of more than a decade. This is what I want you to know: This is an old way of being that could have destroyed my life if I had continued in it.

The same goes for you. If you are currently in the way of being that is destroying your relationships, consider changing your way of being. When I was in a toxic way of being the only one that could not see it was me—surprise! I can't convince you to change; that choice is up to you. What I can say is that my transformation is worth it.

What My Life Looks Like Now

My wife and I have never been closer. She trusts me, something I have never known before, and shares her life with me wholeheartedly. We share faith together, and our love continues to grow. We are both quick to forgive one another and have created space in our relationship to discuss uncomfortable topics. We both had plenty of misconduct in our relationship, and we truly should be divorced. But we have both decided to let the past go and looked forward to a hopeful and bright future. In our relationship, we both own our behavior without blame or excuse. Our relationship has inspired our children, grandchildren, our families, and all of our friends to become the best version of themselves.

Recently, my wife and I traveled to Arizona to visit our son, his family, and especially the grandchildren. My ex-wife was also a part of the visit. During the trip, we had an opportunity with the grandchildren to have a conversation regarding Easter and Christmas. The kids were so enthusiastic about learning.

When we returned from the trip, my wife and I purchased Bibles for each of the grandkids and wrote letters to each of them about how much God loves them. We mailed the books to Arizona. That weekend we received a text from our son explaining how he woke up on a Saturday morning to find the kids entrenched in their Bibles. The text included a picture taken from above, depicting all four grandchildren reading their Bibles.

Now That's Worth It!

Every Labor Day, we are blessed as a family to celebrate in Wisconsin. My brother is a CEO, and his family owns a rather spacious home; it accommodates our entire family, who are blessed with a separate bedroom and bathroom. The home is on a golf course, and the view is relaxing. We also have access to a pool and other country club amenities. Our family has often struggled for time together in the past. Still, in recent years we have realized the importance of spending time together. I am grateful for every moment we share.

When the kids were younger, we lived close to one another; my brother's wife cared for our children while we were working, so our kids grew up together. It is beautiful to experience the way the kids get right back to their closeness. They have an excellent time together. Last year, we were taking the grandchildren along with everyone else to go to a museum. The grandkids were so cute as they broke out in song, singing *Old Town Road*, which I had to record it.

Living life moment to moment and enjoying each one, that's how I live my life now. We are a loving and close family. I remember the days when that was not so, and although I refuse to regret or live in my past, it sure does cause me to be grateful for all my blessings today. I live my life today, knowing every day as an opportunity to make a positive difference in my life and to inspire the same for the people around me.

I am full of love, and people have told me it's contagious. I am quick to forgive and open to the opinions of others. I live my life intentionally, looking for ways to be a part of God's kingdom. I am always on the lookout for opportunities to help people and grow my faith.

"Ask not what your county can do for you, but what you can do for your country."

– John F. Kennedy

As I write this, we as a country are under an executive order to stay home. It is my hope and prayer that, at this time, we draw closer to one another. Before the quarantine, news reports focused primarily on division. "The Democrats are the enemy," or "The Republicans are the enemy." Now that we are faced with a common enemy, I have watched the old news order pass away. I recognize a higher love with my family. I miss those people who I can't be with but acknowledge at this moment that absence does make the heart grow fonder. I miss the Bible studies and other opportunities to serve with my brothers in Christ. Although the possibilities are lost, the love for these people will live on in the years to come.

I look towards a better, healthier, and more grateful nation. It is my hope and prayer that out of this current suffering will emerge a greater love in our country. I stand for faith, for transformation, and new beginnings. Join me in this movement. Hindsight is 2020! Love really does bring us together for a better America. You want to make your life great again, so love in crazy ways and love through hate.

Epilogue

Where Do We Go from Here?

The fear of authoring this book may or may not be evident to you. Nevertheless, the concern is genuine to me. Some people may be offended by my newfound faith. Some may say, "I do not want this book. I need a lawyer who will fight for me." Still, others may laugh at me or make fun of my vulnerabilities. Some may be afraid of their own need for transformation. Regardless of the fears I have faced, I am dedicated to moving forward by selflessly representing individuals and (in many ways) families with a servant's heart.

For those of you who think you need a fierce lawyer, I assure you I am your man. If you have a difficult spouse, who is determined to fight, to hate, to fill their heart with vengeance and untruths, then let me assure you that battling through the process while maintaining your love, forgiveness, and integrity will lead to amazing changes in your life.

Learning to practice law with love, forgiveness, and integrity has changed my life. The transformation I have experienced and continue to experience is impressive. I used to live my life, trying to control everything. When a client's situation went wrong, naturally, the client blamed me. I blamed the court system. Then the client refused to pay the bill. We'd get into a heated battle. I would go home and improperly discipline my children. I would have a massive fight with my wife, which ended in the "divorce" word.

Sound Familiar?

In applying the above facts to my new way of being, love chases away my defensive nature, and I have a productive conversation with my client despite the emotional turmoil. I love my client at that moment, so I can listen to and understand their concerns. I own any responsibility I have in the situation, but I look to hope and a new strategy. If a client lashes out about the bill, I forgive and focus on the client's position. At the end of the discussion, my client will say, "I am sorry, I am just upset," and I indicate, "It is I who am sorry for your situation," and reassure my client that I love them. I am with them to the end.

How Do I Feel When I Come Home?

As I go through my day, it is guaranteed that there will be many conflicts. However, love, forgiveness, and integrity help me to come home with a grateful heart. The disputes I used to carry home, like a 100-pound bag of stinky garbage, are no more. The joys of life are illuminated, and the moments shared as if each one was precious. If you were to ask me, "Why did you write this book," I would answer, "How could I not?" Life never gets brighter than when we are serving others in love.

Here's What You Do Next

If the information in this book gives you hope and shines a light on your pain, in a way that lets you know you don't have to hurt alone, let me help you even more. We can face this together. I will be your guide, and together we will get through this with love, forgiveness, and integrity.

Visit me at http://www.AshandAsh.org.

Recommended Reading:

- Joel Osteen *Your Best Life Now*
- Bob Goff, *Love Does*
- W. P. Young, *The Shack*
- John Ortberg, *The Me I Want to Be*